PRAYERS

TO MY ABBA FATHER

GOD

DAVE CORNELIUS, DM

JCWALK PUBLISHING

Tucson, Arizona

Prayer to my Abba Father God

Copyright © 2019 Dave Cornelius & JCWALK Publishing

Images inspired and provided by Dave Cornelius, DM

JCWALK Publishing

ISBN-13: 978-0-9963936-2-1

PRINTED IN THE UNITED STATES OF AMERICA

Extend the Story: WWW.JCWALK.ORG

CONTENTS

ACKNOWLEDGMENTS

All honor and power and glory be to the creator of all things seen and unseen. Much thanks to my sister Lateefah Collingwood for her contribution to the 10 Things in Love prayer.

Introduction

I began writing these prayers as worship songs to be played, recorded, and shared during church services and other events. In the summer of 2009 on the island of St. Croix in the U.S. Virgin Islands, I shared my book of songs with Pastor Ruben Vessup, a good friend of our family. This is a "Black n' Red" book made in the EU and perhaps 8.5 x 13 in dimension. I still have this book today with an Obama and Biden sticker on it. Pastor Vessup and I sat patiently on my mother's porch as we listened to the birds chirping and the dogs barking, and he declared that these were my prayers. I said to him, no these are my songs that will one day be recorded and played at church services. But he said, these are your prayers and I conceded because Pastor Vessup could argue a point ad nauseum, so I accepted his viewpoint for the time being.

However, I played many of these songs for our worship leader, Dave Pettway, and he declared they were songs of worship. Songs of worship are prayers, so Pastor Vessup and I were both correct in our perspective. Pastor Vessup was a formidable tenor singer and a powerful preacher of the Word. His opinion meant a great deal to me and helped to validate the words that I had written. Sometimes we need a little encouragement to keep us moving forward.

Musicians in the Old Testaments was referred to as Levites. 1 Chronicles 9:33 stated "The musicians, all prominent Levites, lived at the

Temple. They were exempt from other responsibilities since they were on duty at all hours". There is a special place for those given certain creative skills to help others worship God in Spirit and Truth. I have never recorded any of these songs and played a few publicly during worship at Bible studies. My hope is to share these prayers with people who may find them as useful as I have. Perhaps other Levites may want to record and play these songs. That would be an honor to see these prayers as a source of help for others.

GRATITUDE

Gratitude is the spiritual, physical, and emotional space that we are directed to live in and experience daily. Gratitude is derived from the Latin word gratitudinem, which translate to "thankfulness", a deep expression of appreciation for the kindness that we receive from our Abba Father God and people. Observing a person living a life of gratitude is so inspiring, especially when it is Spirit led. You are often paused to ponder what makes them feel the way they feel or demonstrate gratitude with such ease. The behavior is not strained or require much effort. You know that this is a lived experience and not something that happens overnight. I have experienced people demonstrating an attitude of gratitude and you just enjoy being around them. There is always a kind word of encouragement even when you are being guided toward changing a non-productive attitude. This spirit comes from praying to our Abba Father God and developing a deep relationship that is authentic and transparent.

Prayer is asking, expecting, receiving, and responding. Reverence enables our spirit of gratitude to be patient when we ask, expect, receive, and respond with joy and happiness. Joy is the place of spiritual dependence on our Abba Father God to help us navigate the challenges of this world. Happiness depends on things that happens and are often temporary. But when happiness is born in a place blessed by our Abba

Father God it becomes permanent and life changing. Prayer gives us the ability to show gratitude and receive the blessings being poured out of Heavens window.

The following prayers are places and times where my gratitude was expressed in different ways. Some of the places included 1) the beach on St. Croix, U.S.V.I., 2) beaches in Orange County, CA., or 3) the mountains of Tucson, AZ. I have been blessed and have to be grateful for what was given to me, although I could not earn the privilege of the gifts.

Prayer is a conversation with God that begins with gratitude, followed by forgiveness, and then asking how to cooperate with the Kingdom of God on earth. The conversation would go something like:

> Hello Father God, thank you for being my friend and for blessing me with the gifts you have given. Forgive me of my sins (be specific) and I am sorry for falling short today. Help me to understand how I can cooperate with your Holy kingdom on earth by using the gifts you have given me. I welcome the Holy Spirit into my life to pray for me and help me to understand your will. I pray these things in Jesus Name, Amen.

I believe a simple starter prayer like this put our mind and spirit in a place to be able to receive all that God has for us. We begin with humility and acknowledge that we are dependent on God for all that we have. We ask for forgiveness of our sin and are honest about going against the perfect will of God that is best for us. The next step is to ask how we can be helpful in the kingdom of God. Finally, request the help of the Holy Spirit to help us remain connected with God so that we are able to understand things that are beyond our ability to see. Keep things simple as Jesus did. Let me illustrate a simple prayer that Jesus gave to us a few thousand years ago.

Luke 11: 1-2:

> (1) One day Jesus was praying in a certain place. When he was finished, one of his apostles said to him, Lord teach us to pray like John (the Baptist) taught his disciples. Jesus said to them, when you pray, say:

> (2) "Our Father in heaven, Holy be your name.

> Your kingdom come, your will be done, on earth as it is in heaven.

> Give us this day our daily bread, and forgive us our sins, as we forgive those who sin against us.

> And lead us not into temptation but deliver us from evil. Forever Amen"

The power of prayer is beyond words. The relationship that is built with the Creator of all things, people, and spiritual beings and the Savior of this world is a gift. When I pray the Lord's prayer it has very specific meanings and acknowledgements. Prayer is a conversation with God. It is beyond just uttering words in a one-way conversation.

The observation was that Jesus prayed in a certain place. He found a place that he could be without interruptions. Also noted is the apostle waited until Jesus was finished praying before asking him for direction. I can only imagine the mindset of the apostle after witnessing Jesus turn water into wine, heal the sick, and raise people from death, that if he could learn the secret of what Jesus was saying in prayer that he would also have the same capability. I would probably ask for the same advice from Jesus if I was there in that time and was a witness to miracles. Jesus said to the apostles, "when you pray, say". He specifically told them that when and not if they prayed. The expectation was for them to pray in all circumstances good and bad.

The Best Thing (9/26/2008)

Verse:

You gave me hope

Your grace and love

Guided me to the cross

When I was lost

Opened my eyes

To see how beautiful

My life can be

When I live with gratitude

You opened my heart

Filled me with meaning

Gave me everything

I needed

Chorus:

The best thing ever happened to me

Happened to you

Happened when we got his blessings

The best thing ever happened to me

Happened to you

When our hearts needed mending

Verse:

Each day you wake

Me to your will

Lead me to your fields

Filled my hunger and thirst

Cool water runs

Down my face

As I am Baptized in your love

Accepted in your family

Joy and gladness

Found everywhere

Thankful songs

Fill the air

Chorus:

The best thing ever happened to me

Happened to you

Happened when we got his blessings

The best thing ever happened to me

Happened to you

When our hearts needed mending

Bridge:

I've got everything You promised

So grateful for my blessings

Delivered, Uplifted

Your favor rains down on me

Jesus Christ (JC's) Way (4/6/2007)

Verse:

My walk is getting stronger

It was just yesterday

I was living a life filled with rage

He showed me the way

Eternity is longer

More than life and money you crave

Forget about temporary things

Seek Heaven instead

It's not easy to walk JC's way

Wrap yourself in His love and pray

Let His word live in your heart today

And be freed

It's not easy to love JC's way

Forgiving those who hate your face

He gave His life and took your place

Now I'm free

Chorus:

Be joyful always

Pray continuously

Be glad in all things

It's His will for you

Be always thankful

Serve with gladness

Fruit of the Spirit

Love, joy, and kindness

Verse:

Pray by the Spirit

I'm free to accept His grace

When you live by faith, life is given

The fruit of my father

Born to be a witness

Born to praise the risen King

Free at last, from chains of past

The bondage is broken

It's not easy to walk JC's way

Wrap yourself in His love and pray

Let His word live in your heart today

And be freed

It's not easy to love JC's way

Forgiving those who hate your face

He gave His life and took your place

Now I'm free

Repeat Chorus:

Dear God (4/12/2007)

Verse:

Thank you for this day

Another chance to live on

Your love reflects this way

Anointing me

Surrender all I am

All the things of the day

Bless my fellow man

Help them see and understand

Chorus:

Dear God

What you've planned for me today?

My God

I'll get out of the way

Dear God

I'll listen for your word today

My God

I hear what you have to say

Verse:

Forgive me for my will

And my prideful ways

I'll seek you and be still

Rescue me from sin

Let me know your will

Strengthen me to go on

You know everything

Your grace and mercy lift me up

Repeat Chorus:

Full of the Spirit (5/2/2007)

Verse:

Now the burden is lifted

He's always with me

My friend, my Father, my Savior

The Trinity

Where can you find love, pure love

Abundantly

Where can you feel loved, so loved

Only through Jesus

Precious Jesus

Chorus:

I'm full of His Spirit

Holy Spirit

Graced with His love

I'm full of His Spirit

Powerful Spirit

Transformed my life

I'm full of His Spirit

Fruits of the Spirit

Power and joy

15

I'm full of His Spirit

Heavenly Spirit

Perfect and good

Verse:

You go before me and stand behind me

Your hand blessed my head

Such knowledge too wonderful for me

Too great to understand

Search me God and know my heart

Test me and know my thoughts

Lead me along your path

To everlasting life

Repeat Chorus:

Jesus Died for You and Me (5/10/2007)

Verse:

They didn't believe

He was the Messiah

Wanted to Kill

The son of the Father

But He already knew

Man can be so cruel

Judas betrayed

The King and Savior

Peter Denied

Three times he knew Him

He predicted this time

He would be denied

By those who knew him

Those He had chosen

Chorus:

Jesus died for you and me

Gave His life

To cleanse our sins

His love is so great

Can we comprehend?

Salvation is yours

If you want it

Jesus died for you and me

Gave His life

Cleansed our sins

Faith in Him

Is all we need

Eternity is yours

If you want it

Verse:

Thorns in His head

Cross on His shoulder

Flogged with whips of lead

Mocked by soldiers

What a sacrifice

The way, the truth, the life

Placed on the cross

Nails in His feet and hands

They threw the dice

Divided His garments

Father forgive them

I will come again

Send the Holy Spirit

To guide us

Repeat Chorus:

Live Today (6/27/2008)

Verse:

He made me perfect

In His likeness

Higher than Angels

To join Him one day

When the Christ comes again

Poured out His blessings

From the windows of Heaven

A gift of His presence

A full and fruitful life

Want to know your will

Chorus:

I live today

Guided by His goodness

Walking in His light

In Christ

I live Today

Thankful for His blessings

The apple of His eyes

Verse:

He made me to love me

To last forever

Eternity together

This life in your son

I accept you in my life again today

Delivered from darkness

Transferred to His Kingdom

I present my body

Living sacrifice

To glorify your name

Repeat Chorus:

When We Get to Heaven (7/4/2008)

Verse:

When we get to Heaven

There will be joy and singing

Our reward will be given

For how we lived our lives

I won't be missing

All the lies we're given

No temptation

From the flesh or evil one

Chorus:

I can't wait until we get to Heaven

All God's faithful servants

Will be crowned

I can't wait until we get to Heaven

We'll be free

From all the sins on earth

Verse:

We'll be permitted

Through the gates of the city

Eat the fruit

From the tree of life

If we desire

We can drink freely

From the water of life

If we kept the faith in him

Repeat Chorus:

Trust in the Lord (7/08/2008)

Verse:

When you're lost

In the crowd

And it seems

So very long

When you can't find

Your way

Jesus will guide you

Into His loving arms

Chorus:

Trust in the Lord

For all of your needs

When things are good

When they are bad

Let Him lead your plans

Carry your load

Trust in the Lord

And be anointed

Trust in the Lord

To heal all your hurts

Focus your thoughts

On His promises

Tell Him your problems

And be freed from your strain

Trust in the Lord

And be uplifted

Verse:

When you feel

You're been given too much

A heavy burden

Weighing down on you

If your heart is in doubt

You are never given more

Than you can stand

Repeat Chorus:

I've Got Redemption (7/10/2008)

Verse:

I've got redemption

A gift from the Lord

All I had to do

Was to accept Him as my Savior

All my sins

Forgiven

Because He loved me while

I was a sinner

It doesn't take good deeds

Just faith in Christ the Lord

Although it pays

To help those in need

Open your heart

And give to receive

You will be blessed

More than you can see

Chorus:

I've got Redemption (I am redeemed)

I've got Redemption (I am alive in Him)

I've got Redemption (Saved by His grace)

Call on His name

You will be saved

Verse:

I saw a family

Huddled on the street

All of their things

Were tossed into bags

On my heart

It was spoken

Share the treasures

I have given you

That's when I knew

That the Lord worked through me

I was doubtful

So I began to pray

I got this feeling

That things would be alright

Whatever He blesses

Never fails

Repeat Chorus:

Miracle in Motion (8/09/2008)

Verse:

I prayed and started my day

Grabbed the full armor of God

Another hectic day

So hold on

You will be tested

Again, and again, and again

It's a spiritual warfare

Stand your ground

Stand firm

Take up the shield of faith

Put the belt of truth

Around your waist

Thank you

For this time

To love and serve

All your little saints

I may not be ready

Because I never had to do this before

Chorus:

Miracle in motion

With love and devotion

See the love of Jesus

Alive in their eyes

Miracle in motion

Love on all God's children

Share the work of Jesus

Into their lives

Verse:

See those flaming arrows

Heading for my heart

Put them out again

Before they wreck my heart

And twist my mind

Now I'm ready

To stand the test

Share my love and Joy

With open arms

With all God's little saints

Thank you

For this chance

To love and serve

All your little saints

I may not be ready

Because I never had to do this before

Repeat Chorus:

He Gave Me Life (9/12/2008)

Verse:

You gave me life

Know who I'd be

Laid out your plan

As you shaped me

In my mother's womb

The mystery of life

Made by your hands

You breathe life in me

Who should I thank?

My mom or dad?

Or it is the hand of God in the plan

One thing I know

He spoke and the world came to be

So, He made me

Chorus:

He gave me life

To love me

He gave me life

To glorify Him

He gave me life

To praise Him

He gave me life

A-men

Verse:

I hear them ask

When does life start?

I say it's when God gives life

Knitted in my mother's womb

Wonderfully complex

His work is so great

Marvelously made

In His likeness

One of His children

He's my rock and my salvation

Placed in my heart

A vision that I was made to live for eternity

Gave me the gift of faith

Love in my heart

Fruits of the Spirit

So wonderful

Repeat Chorus:

Bridge:

Life did not start by chance

It was the voice of God

He said, let there be life

And there was life

He gave me the greatest gift of all

Repeat Chorus:

Share The Word (9/20/2008)

Verse:

Messenger of the good news, shout it

Shout it louder to your brother

The word of God stands forever

From the beginning to the end

Live in His Word

Walk by His word

Write it in your heart

Store it in your mind

Continue what Jesus started

Seek and save the lost

Chorus:

Share the Word with everyone you meet

And start His revolution

Share the Word and see His work in lives

That need an evolution

Verse:

We listen every day to His words of wisdom

We sing and shout His praise

Lift our hands and voices

Read His Word and you will see the changes

In your life each day

In the Words you pray

Live in His Word

Walk by His word

Write it in your heart

Store it in your mind

Continue what Jesus started

Seek and save the lost

Repeat Chorus:

Bridge:

With You

All things are possible

With you

My cup overflows

With You

There's light in my life

So, I will

Repeat Chorus:

I Will Sing (11/27/2010)

Verse:

Chant a Psalm a day

Meditate on its meaning

Let the wisdom of Proverbs

Guide me through the day

All I need to know

Was written long ago

Put down my will and follow

Where I'm led to go

Chorus:

I will sing, song of songs

Sing of His love

Flowing over me

I will sing, sing His songs

Lift up my voice

To celebrate you now

Verse:

I appreciate what you have done for me

Removed the scales so I can see

The beauty of your majesty

In the Trinity

I am strengthened by your walk

I witness, I sing and shout

Jesus, Jesus

Thank you for saving me

Repeat Chorus:

Bridge:

Everything you do

Is beautiful to me

Wonderfully, majestically done

Everything you say

Resonate in me

All because of your son

He gave life where there was none

Repeat Chorus:

Jesus Who Saves Us (10/14/2008)

Verse:

People wonder why I'm full of joy

Always giving thanks for everything

I was given the gift of faith

That I may have salvation

Chorus:

Jesus

The only one who saves us

Holy and righteous

Call me His Friend

Jesus

The living Word that change us

Gives His love and wisdom

The only true God

Verse:

He has changed my life in every way

Help to endure the best today

Patience and love to obey

That I may be forgiven

All I had to do was ask Him

Come into my life

Accept Him as my savior

By His grace, I am saved

Repeat Chorus:

Teach Me to Love (10/30/2008)

Intro:

La La La La_

La_ La La La_

La La La La_

Verse:

Break down the walls that keep us apart

Fill me with your love and cleanse my heart

I will surrender completely

And be devoted

Draw closer to you

Chorus:

Teacher

Teach me to love you each day

More and More everyday

As I walk in your light

Touched by your life

Show me

Show me your love each day

More and more everyday

I am cloaked in your love

Renewed in life

Verse:

Scatter the things that keep us apart

Mend our fences with love from the start

Embrace each other

In Unity

Brothers and sisters in Christ

Repeat Chorus:

Take Up Your Cross, Follow Me (10/31/2008)

Verse:

Put down your will, take up my cause

Put your selfish ways on pause

If you want to live, take hold of me

Give up your life for my sake

What would you gain, if you lose your soul?

What would you gain, nothing at all?

What is worth more than your soul

Not even the whole world in your hands

Chorus:

Take up your cross and follow me

I can give everything to make you complete

Take up your cross and follow me

Be my disciple and bear fruit in my name

Verse:

Abide in my word, be one with me

I'm the maker of truth, to set you free

If you are ashamed of the Good news

I'll turn my back on you in the end

What would you gain, if you lose your soul?

What would you gain, nothing at all?

What is worth more than your soul

Not even the whole world in your hands

Chorus:

Take up your cross and follow me

I can give everything to make you complete

Take up your cross and follow me

Be my disciple and bear fruit in my name

I'm Blessed (11/08/2008)

Verse:

Oh oh oh

How do you feel today? You say I'm blessed

Oh oh oh

When things are upside down? You say I'm blessed

Oh oh oh

When disaster strikes? You say I'm blessed

I am blessed

I am blessed to know you

I am blessed you chose me

I am so thankful

Chorus:

I am blessed in life

I am blessed today

I am blessed to know that you love me

I am blessed in life

I am blessed today

I am blessed to know that you want me forever

Verse:

Oh oh oh

When things are going alright? You say I'm blessed

Oh oh oh

When your prayers are answered? You say I'm blessed

Oh oh oh

When you bear fruit for him? You say I'm blessed

I am blessed

I am blessed to know you

I am blessed you chose me

I am so thankful

Repeat Chorus:

Won't Walk in Circles (11/29/2008)

Verse:

Every night I close my eyes

Fall into a deep sleep

Wake up in the morning

Knowing you are with me

Got joy and peace in me

A witness for all to see

Bearing fruit abundantly

Guided by the hand of royalty

Royalty above all else

Paved the way so

Chorus:

I won't walk in circles

Chase the world

Feeling so restless

Singing, mm, mm, nah, nah, nah, nah, nah, nah

Won't walk in circles

Chase the world

Feeling so restless

Singing, mm, mm, nah, nah, nah, nah, nah, nah

Verse:

So, I think I have got it down

Preachin', servin' through the town

Heard His voice said

Stop what you are doing and follow me right now

I was blind now I see

Paved the way so

Repeat Chorus:

Bridge:

So, I'll live my life

As the salt and light of this world

I'll shine my light before

Wear it on my sleeves and shoulder

Welcome to My House (12/6/2008)

Verse:

Welcome everyone

Come and get some of this

Love that never fades away

Come and raise your hands

Lift your voices

Praise Him like you truly care

Come let's meet together

Give and share our treasures

Embrace and love each other everyday

Encourage one another

In every way

Chorus:

Welcome to my house

Where the harvest of His love is ripe

Welcome to my house

The sweetness of the Word, renews your heart

Welcome to my house

There are many rooms in my Father's house

Verse:

Welcome everyone

Come and get some of this

Love that never fades away

Come and raise your hands

Lift your voices

Praise Him like you truly care

Come let's meet together

Give and share our treasures

Embrace and love each other everyday

Encourage each other

In every way

Chorus:

Welcome to my house

Where the harvest of His love is ripe

Welcome to my house

The sweetness of the Word, renews your heart

Welcome to my house

There are many rooms in my Father's house

Bridge:

There are blessings in this place

Refuge and His Grace

Many are invited to the wedding banquet

There are blessings in this house

Clap your hands and shout

Where there is two or more of us

Come let's meet together

Give and share our treasures

Encourage each other

In every way

Verse:

Welcome to our house

Our hearts are filled with joy

Love that never fades away

Our arms are open wide

You are always welcome

Into the house of A-do-nai

Come let's meet together

Give and share our treasures

Embrace and love each other everyday

Encourage each other

In every way

Repeat Chorus:

Fall on Me (12/20/2008)

Verse:

You gave me hope that I can build

Your Kingdom in me

You cause all things to work together

For those who love

I am strengthened, have no fear

Unshaken I'll be

You cause all things to work together for those who love you

And I'll lean on you

Pray to you

Walk with you

All things work together

For those who love You

Chorus:

Fall on

Fall on

Let your love fall on my Lord

Let your wisdom fall on me

Fall on

Fall on

Let your joy fall on me Lord

Let your love fall on me

Verse:

You gave me hope that I can build

Your Kingdom in me

You cause all things to work together

For those who love

I am strengthened, have no fear

Unshaken I'll be

You cause all things to work together for those who love you

And I'll lean on you

Pray to you

Walk with you

All things work together

For those who love You

Chorus:

Fall on

Fall on

Let your love fall on my Lord

Let your wisdom fall on me

Fall on

Fall on

Let your joy fall on me Lord

Let your love fall on me

Bridge:

Fall on, Fall on

Let the Manna hidden in Heaven

Fall on, Fall on

Everyone who lives for you

Fall on, Fall on

Let the Manna hidden in Heaven

Fall on, Fall on

Victorious we live for you

10 Things in Love (12/23/2008)

Verse:

A love story, guided by the one who strengthens us

An attitude of gratitude for all our blessings

Clothed ourselves with tender hearted humility

A giving heart that is the eyes of love

A stillness of mind knowing you are always here

Chorus:

There are 10 things I want in love

A gift from the one in Heaven above

There are 10 things I want in love

I pray for each day

Come fill my heart with joy and love always

Verse:

To walk hand in hand with you

I always feel secure

A heart that's open to the least of these

Your Word as our center, leading us through each moment

Open arms to serve and show His loving grace

A light shining bright for all the world to see

Chorus:

There are 10 things I want in love

A gift from the one in Heaven above

There are 10 things I want in love

I pray for each day

Come fill my heart with joy and love always

You're My #1 (1/11/2009)

Verse:

Every day I want to live

My life the way you did

Sharing love, sharing hope

Plant the seeds and watch them grow

In my heart, in my mind

Lift my spirit and transform mine now

You give abundantly in love

Chorus:

You're my #1 and I lift you higher

You're my #1 you set my heart on fire

You're my #1 I've got so much love for you

Come on sing along, praise the Messiah

You're my #1, you are all I desire

You're my #1 you set my heart on fire

You're my #1 I've got so much love for you

Come on sing along, praise the Messiah

Verse:

If I could see the world

Through your eyes, the way that you do

Share your joy, share your peace

Plant the seeds and watch them grow

In my heart, in my mind

Lift my spirit and transform mine now

You give abundantly in love

Chorus:

You're my #1 and I lift you higher

You're my #1 you set my heart on fire

You're my #1 I've got so much love for you

Come on sing along, praise the Messiah

You're my #1, you are all I desire

You're my #1 you set my heart on fire

You're my #1 I've got so much love for you

Come on sing along, praise the Messiah

Only You (1/20/2009)

Verse:

Sometimes I wonder, why you comfort us

Sometimes I wonder, why you care

But you

Left the highest place above

To be in the lowest place with us

Became a servant to all

Even though you are the King

Chorus:

Only you can dry the tears of my heart

Only you knew the end from the start

Only you are the light in the dark

Only you give me joy

Only you hear the noise in my mind

Only you help me see when I am blind

Only you give me strength to last

Only you all the time

Verse:

You kept your promise to deliver us

You placed your kingdom in our hearts

From His high and Holy place

Touched our hearts, revealed your love

Gave us your wisdom and your truth

To give us victory

Rejoice in the Lord

Chorus:

Only you can dry the tears of my heart

Only you knew the end from the start

Only you are the light in the dark

Only you give me joy

Only you hear the noise in my mind

Only you help me see when I am blind

Only you give me strength to last

Only you all the time

Will You Love Me? (2/11/2009)

Verse:

The first and greatest command is for you

To love me with all of your heart and soul

With all of your mind

And all of your strength

That's what I ask of you

The second and greatest command is for you

To love your brothers and sisters

As you love yourself

Love each other

That's what I ask

Chorus:

Will you love me

Love me today

Will you love me

The way I love you

Will you love me

With kindness and joy

Will you love me

Because of my love

The joy I give

The way I love you

Because of who I am

Verse:

My love is perfect

The best you can get

Unconditionally

Lasting forever

I don't need a reason

To love you today

That's what I give

My love is giving

In abundance it flows

My love restores, mends, and heals

I pour out my love

Into you

That's what I give

Chorus:

Will you love me

Love me today

Will you love me

The way I love you

Will you love me

With kindness and joy

Will you love me

Because of my love

The joy I give

The way I love you

Because of who I am

Place of Worship (5/3/2009)

Verse:

Worship to God's revelation

The fruits of my lips are praise

The fruits of my life are worship revival

Pour out a drink offering in worship

Be poured out in praise

Chorus:

Keep me in this place of worship

Live in your Word

Forgive them all

Come do your work in me

Keep me in the place of worship

I'll praise your name

Rejoice in love

Submit my life to you

Revelation is here

Verse:

Worship, giving my first fruits

Surrendered is a heart of worship

Delivered in His house of worship

Pour out a drink offering in worship

Be poured out in praise

Chorus:

Keep me in this place of worship

Live in your Word

   Forgive them all

   Come do your work in me

   Keep me in the place of worship

   I'll praise your name

   Rejoice in love

   Submit my life to you

   Revelation is here

Bridge:

I will always worship you

With the blessing you placed in me

I'll live a life of worship

To release your light flowing through me

I will always worship you

Pour out my life in praise, in service

I'll live a life of worship

To release your light flowing through me

Today (6/7/2009)

Verse:

What if today is your last

And our redeemer came

For the citizens to dwell in Heaven's gate

For those who lived His Word, glorify His Name

Go and love completely

Live life with integrity

Forgive those who trespass against you

Every day, for everything

Chorus:

Today

Live today as your last

Today

Give to those when they ask

Build your house on solid foundation

On the rock of salvation

Verse:

How will you live your dash?

Will it be intentional

Will you hear them say you fought the good fight

You finished the race, you have kept the faith

Go and love completely

Live life with integrity

Forgive those who trespass against you

Every day, for everything

Chorus:

Today

Live today as your last

Today

Give to those when they ask

Build your house on solid foundation

On the rock of salvation

You Rescued Me Again (9/23/2009)

Verse:

In my distress I pray to you

You heard my cries and answered me

Answered me

Even when I fall

Short of your will for me

You rescued me again and again

In a great fish

Deep in the seas

My prayer rose to you

And you answered me

Even when I fall

Short of your will for me

Let it be your will

I will hold the cup

Strengthen me again

So that I

May give you praise

In everything I do

Everything I say

A song of praise

Chorus:

You rescued me again

You said you'd love me to the end

Surrender and submit my life to you

To give praise and glory

You rescued me again

You embrace me as your friend

I can feel your love renewing me

I was made to live with you forever

Verse:

In my distress I pray to you

You heard my cries and answered me

Answered me

Even when I fall

Short of your will for me

You rescued me again and again

In a great fish

Deep in the seas

My prayer rose to you

And you answered me

Even when I fall

Short of your will for me

Let it be your will

I will hold the cup

Strengthen me again

So that I

May give you praise

In everything I do

Everything I say

A song of praise

Chorus:

You rescued me again

You said you'd love me to the end

Surrender and submit my life to you

To give praise and glory

You rescued me again

You embrace me as your friend

I can feel your love renewing me

I was made to live with you forever

Bridge:

You are the only Sovereign God

Who was and is and is to come

Holy is the Lord God almighty

The Lord God almighty

Holy, Holy, Hallelujah

Such A Joy (9/24/2009)

It is such a joy to be your child

It is such a joy to call you Dad

It is such a joy to live life with you

Abba, Father, God, your love is Divine

It is such a joy to praise your name

It is such a joy to pray to you

It is such a joy to love in your name

Abba, Father, God, your love is Divine

Abba, Father, God, your love is Divine

The Lord blesses you

And He keeps you

The Lord make His face

Shine upon you

He is gracious to you

And will always love you

The Lord turn His face toward you

And give you peace

The Living Water (7/31/2010)

Verse:

I met a man

With holes in his hands

Holes in His feet

And in His right side

He told me His name

And changed the game

Things will never, ever be the same

Blessed are those who believe

Have not seen me

Blessed are those who believe

Have received me

Chorus:

Come and drink from the living water

From your heart the river flows

Come and drink from the living water

Living streams will flow

Come and drink from the living water

From the deep never thirst again

Come and drink from the living water

Living streams will flow

Verse:

I met a man

With a crown of thorns

On the crown of His head

He told he came

To release me from blame

I heavy debt I could never repay

Blessed are those who believe

Have not seen me

Blessed are those who believe

Have received me

Chorus:

Come and drink from the living water

From your heart the river flows

Come and drink from the living water

Living streams will flow

Come and drink from the living water

From the deep never thirst again

Come and drink from the living water

Living streams will flow

Bridge:

Spring of living water

Welling up to eternal life

Spring of living water

You will never be thirsty again

It's A Perfect Day (10/9/2010)

Verse:

The love in His Story

Renew this broken life

I know how much you love me

I claim your promises

Why would you love this broken child constantly?

You lift me out of darkness, now I am free

I pray continuously

I will pray continuously

Uplifted in prayer, Holy prayer

I will pray continuously

Chorus:

It's a perfect day, I'm in His glory

It's a perfect day, to live His story

Share it throughout the land

It's a perfect day, for a revelation

It's a perfect day, for salvation

Share it throughout the land

WANDERING

We wander physically, emotionally, and spiritually. Our spirits are restless as we live in the time of now and not yet. The Kingdom of God is here but not fully realized. What trying times that we live in today? The story of the Israelites wandering in the desert for 40 years when the journey from Egypt to the land of Canaan was just 11 days. This a 132727% increase or 1,327 more time lost than was expected. What drifters we are! Ever try to meditate and keep your mind focused for more than 5-minutes? Such a struggle, even when practiced. The ability to stay on the straight and narrow path is challenging and we fall off many times. But the goal is to keep trying to get back on the path no matter how many times we drift into a path that is not beneficial for our eternal life and spirit. Spiritual wandering is nothing new, people have suffered from this affliction from the beginning of time. The story of Adam and Eve is a perfect example of spiritual wandering. Two people able to walk and talk with God at any time traded a mountain and ocean view for a garbage dump. They traded the right to have everything for a glimpse of nothing beneficial. We wander spiritually because there are forces that fight to control our destination and we have the option to say no thank you, eternity in Heaven is so much better. It is not always easy but there is nothing wrong with putting up a good fight and not surrendering to receive less than we are entitled.

The remedies for spiritual wandering begin with prayer to our Abba Father God. When we find an attractive distraction that will take us in opposition to God's will for us, it is time to pray for guidance and encouragement. Fame, lust, food, and our own will are a few that comes to mind. The second remedy is sharing the Word of God with others that you meet. This is not about standing on the street corner shouting at people but genuinely sharing your personal experience with your Abba Father God's favor in your life. The third is to stay the course and remain on the straight and narrow path of righteousness. I used to be a cigar and cigarette smoker and at times those craving will come along when things are either going well or I am experiencing challenges. My spirit quickly reminds me that I was not given a spirit of weakness but was made in the likeness of God. God does not want me to pollute the temple where the Holy Spirit resides.

The prayers written in the following pages are a reflection of my struggle with spiritual wandering in the early days of walking with Jesus. I must admit even today, I still struggle with spiritual wandering. Even the well-seasoned pastors and followers of Jesus suffer with spiritual wandering. It is an epidemic that draws us into living a life of sin, which is to be opposite to God's perfect will for us.

Heaven is Silent (5/10/2007)

Verse:

Heaven is silent

Will you follow me

Test your faith, unchanged

Walk without seeing

Believe without receiving

Heavy loads

Unguided steps

Falling on your face

Asking for your presence

Come and fill my loneliness

I haven't heard from you

Will you show your face

Your servant needs you

You won't abandon me

Your promise is always true

Chorus:

Heaven is silent, He's listening

Praise him everyday

Rely on Him for everything

Call on His name

Heaven is silent, He's listening

When you're fumbling in the dark

Keep on living by faith

Keep on giving Him praise

Verse:

Feel His presence

Live in victory

Knowing His truth

Freedom rewarded

And be encouraged

Job lived faithfully

Yet, lost everything

What would you do?

If you walked in his shoes

Cry out for His light

Take away this darkness

That surrounds me

His word tells us

To live the truth, we know

Repeat Chorus:

I'm Not Alone (2/6/2009)

Verse:

When I walk in the valley

In the shadow of light

I can feel my heart racing

In your delight

I'm not afraid

You walk with me

Comfort me

You are my Shepherd

I don't need a thing

Refreshing waters

A quiet pool to drink

Refreshes my spirit

True to your word

I am filled with your breath

Chorus:

I'm not alone

I'm not on my own I know

You sent me right

When I want to go left

You whisper wisdom

When I'm foolish and deaf

Your beauty and love chase me

Each day

I'm not alone, I'm not alone, I'm not alone

Verse:

You prepare a table

In front of my foes

Willing and able

Anointed my head

With your oil of favor

My cup is full

Overflowing

Surely goodness and love

Will follow me all my days

I will dwell in His favor

Throughout my years

Growing and faithful

Trusting in you

Joyful and thankful

Chorus:

I'm not alone

I'm not on my own

I know

You sent me right

When I want to go left

You whisper wisdom

When I'm foolish and deaf

Your beauty and love chase me

Each day

I'm not alone, I'm not alone, I'm not alone

Lead Me (9/11/2008)

Verse:

When I wake up in the morning

Through the journey of the day

As I earn my daily bread

When I sow the seeds of love

When I'm hungry and I'm tired

When I am broken down in tears

You lift me up and bless me

With your love I want to live

Each day to glorify your Holy Name

Chorus:

Lead me, Lord

Use me, Lord

I am your faithful servant

Go before me

Shine your light on me

Lead, me, Lord

Use me, Lord

From the morning

To the night

I'll live in your house

All the days of my life

Verse:

Through the troubles that I can't see

The light at the end of the tunnel

Your greatness is so wonderful

I can't find the words to say

When I live my life

As a witness of your transformation in me

You lift me up and bless me

With your love I want to live

Each day to glorify your Holy Name

Chorus:

Lead me, Lord

Use me, Lord

I am your faithful servant

Go before me

Shine your light on me

Lead, me, Lord

Use me, Lord

From the morning

To the night

I'll live in your house

All the days of my life

Bridge:

Wash me clean

Purify me

Give me joy forever

Now let me rejoice

In your Holy Name

When We're In Heaven (3/31/2014)

Chorus:

I pray everyday

Appealing to your grace, asking

When will you come?

When will you come?

So, I can be with you

I pray everyday

Singing of your Holiness, praying

When will you come?

When will you come?

For us to worship with you

Verse:

When we're in Heaven

There will be no pain

When we're in Heaven

Our tears are wiped away

When we're in Heaven

Our joy will be with you

When we're in Heaven

All Things are made new

Verse:

When we're in Heaven

Our thirst will be quenched

When we're in Heaven

We will drink the water of life

When we're in Heaven

Our joy will be with you

When we're in Heaven

All Things are made new

I'll Hang On In There (11/6/2010)

Hello Savior, it's me

Where are you?

I've been waiting so long

To be with you

I'll hang on in there

Hang on in there patiently

Hello Healer, I'm here

Seeking you

I see your love in creation

Shining through

I'll hang on in there

Hang on in there till you come

I've packed my bags

Waiting for you

Don't know the day or hour of your return

So, I must keep watch

Store my treasures in Heaven

I'll hang on in there

Hang on in there

Hang on in there

Hang on in there till you come

Hello redeemer, I'm free

Because of you

The light you shine within me

For the chosen few

I'll hang on in there

Hang on in there patiently

Hello Creator

Creation groans for you

I hear the crying for you

To make all things new

I'll hang on in there

Hang on in there till you come

Rescue Me (9/20/2009)

Rescue me

Save me from myself

Desires of the flesh

The pleasures of sin

Won't you rescue me?

Release the stronghold

Of the strong man

Deceiving my temple

Give me the strength

The armor of the Lord

The shield of faith

Please rescue me

Don't let them win

Make me your witness

My mouth boldly sing praise

Let it be your will

I will hold the cup

Strengthen me again

So that I

May give you praise

Do You Know (11/27/2008)

Verse:

Do you know your purpose?

Do you know why you are here?

Do you know?

Do you know your purpose?

Do you sit and wonder?

What happens when you go under?

Do you know? Do you know?

Do you know your fate?

Chorus:

What do we have to do?

Just fix our gaze on Jesus

What do you have to say?

Thank you for the change you placed in me

Verse:

Tell me you are ready

Tell me you are safe

Do you know? Do you know?

Do you know your purpose?

Can you see the future?

Can you see your fate?

Do you know? Do you know?

Do you know your fate?

Chorus:

What do we have to do?

Just fix our gaze on Jesus

What do you have to say?

Thank you for the change you placed in me

Bridge:

One thing is certain

His love can move mountains

Restores what is broken

Do you know? Do you know?

BE STILL

To be still requires discipline and patience to remain in quietness and wait for the voice of God to direct your next move. My nature is to be active - whether I am shaking my legs, tapping my fingers, or counting spaces on the wall, it is the wonderful and beautiful way that I was made. So I ask why are we commanded in Psalms 46:10 to "Be still and know that I am God"?

Psalms 46: 10:

He says, "Be still, and know that I am God;

I will be exalted among the nations,

I will be exalted in the earth."

What comes to mind is that we often forget to acknowledge God for all He has done for us. Perhaps we can look at it in terms of find peace so we can make space for God to bring goodness in your life. Most people are not able to be still without practice. My mind is a very busy place and often want to be filled with exciting or mind-numbing experiences. Even in prayer, a place where I want to be still, it is difficult to remain still. However, it is a call for us to reflect on what God can do when we are not capable or lack the ability.

Be still is a meditative state that we use to pause what is going on around us to acknowledge that God is alpha and omega in all things. This means our busy day with family, work, hobbies, friends, and much more. Each morning when you wake up from sleep, it is time to be still and give thanks for another day of life. Throughout the day pause and give thanks to God for the simple things. Each night before you lay your head down to sleep, be still and intentionally give thanks for another day of learning.

When we are still, we have the opportunity to dream about eternity with our Abba Father God. We live in a noisy time where distractions are easy. We have devices that vibrate, beep, chime, and demand that we pay attention to the content being pushed at us. My preference is to use my mobile or tablet device for my Bible, but at times, I pick up my Bible and use that for meditation. I can drown out the noise even when using an electronic device but there are times when my spirit needs mending and my NLT student Bible is the answer.

I pray the words that I was inspired to write helps with identifying areas in your life that requires stillness. The words that follows are my prayers that I experienced in situations requiring me to be still and know that God was present. We have to stop striving and moving to realize that God is in control and truly His name is exalted in the nations and in the earth.

Be Still (7/14/2010)

Verse:

In the desert wandering

Dependent on your Grace

Manna falling

Hear you calling

Come into my rest

In the wilderness I grumble

Wait on me, be humble

I'm about to do, something new

See, I have already began

Your Latter will be greater

Be faithful

Chorus:

Be still

And know that I am God

Who always love you

Be still

And know that I'm the God of Grace

I have plans to prosper you

Not harm you

Plans to give you hope and a future

Then you will call upon me

Come and pray to me

I will listen to you

Be still and know that I'm God

God Is (9/13/2010)

Verse:

The bird of the air

Do not sow, or reap, or store away

Yet the Father shows them

Favor and feed them

We are worth more

And created in His likeness

Unconstrained in His mercy

Chorus:

God is so able

He gives a sinner endless life

God is so loving

Loving us every day and every night

God is so Holy

Holy, Holy, Holy

God is so worthy

The beginning and the end

Verse:

Extend your hands

To receive the power of healing

Be unchained from bondage

Bow your heads

Give Him praise in humble worship

Unconstrained in His mercy

Chorus:

God is so able

He gives a sinner endless life

God is so loving

Loving us every day and every night

God is so Holy

Holy, Holy, Holy

God is so worthy

The beginning and the end

Agape Is Love You Cannot Repay (1/13/2011)

Chorus:

I don't know how to receive love

So, I don't know how to love in return

I know it's more than emotional feelings

Agape is love you cannot repay

I don't love you as I should now

Maybe my heart is in the wrong place again

I know to trust you will fill me with love

Agape is love you cannot repay

Verse:

I'll start my day with your sweet songs

Keeping you close deep inside

Cry out with joy for your constant grace

I live for the day when we're face to face

Verse:

If I have done great things but have not love

Then I am nothing at all

How sweet it is, I know how it ends

Together with you, I rejoice to the end

I don't love you as I should now

Maybe my heart is in the wrong place again

I know to trust you will fill me with love

Agape is love you cannot repay

(Without) His Love (9/28/2008)

Verse:

Without His love

I would be stuck in my sin

Be a slave to the law

But I'm not perfect

So, He sent His Son

To stand in my place

What would be my faith?

Without His Grace

He gives faith and love

Hope and love

Love is the greatest

Of them all

He gives faith and love

Hope and love

Love is the greatest

Of them all

Can you see your life without Him?

Can you live your life without Him?

Can you see your life without Him?

Can you live your life without Him?

Verse:

Without His love

I would be hopeless and lost

There would be not joy

I would be broken hearted

I am grateful each day

For the gift of my faith

I did not earn this

But for His Grace

His goodness and love

He gives faith and love

Hope and love

Love is the greatest

Of them all

He gives faith and love

Hope and love

Love is the greatest

Of them all

Can you see your life without Him?

Can you live your life without Him?

Can you see your life without Him?

Can you live your life without Him?

In Your Name (9/20/2010)

Verse:

Let me walk with you in truth

All things absolute

Meditate in solitude

Only in your name

I hear the life-giving words and I see the miracles

I feel the love you give to me

Only in your name

There is no one else who can

make the whole world saints to stand with you, praise you

Chorus:

In your name

I can find meaning

In your name

I know my purpose

In your name

You are my portion

In your name

There is joy and power

Verse:

Hold firmly to the word of life in you

I want to share that joy of Christ with you

Shine like the stars in the universe

Become blameless and pure

Saints to stand with you, praise you

Hear What I Say (7/30/2010)

Verse:

Meditate on me today

Meditate on me, pray

On bended knees, reverently

Intercede with groans for me

Intercede with groans for me

That words cannot express

I wait patiently

You don't have to say a word

Pour out your heart to me

You don't have to say a word

Put your trust in me

Come as you are

Broken, ashamed, without a cent

Desperately, lean on me

Chorus:

Will you stop to pray?

Hear what I have to say

Give it all away

Give it all away

Will you come

Lay your weary head

Beside the still waters

Peace in my rest

In the green pastures

Hear what I say

Humility (1/1/2009)

Verse:

It's not about you

It's not about me

Starts with the One, the beginning, the end

Everything in life starts with Him

Find its purpose in Him

Life is greater

When you humbly walk with Him

So much greater

When you have a humble heart

Chorus:

Humility

Shows when He has a hold on me

Spirituality

Needs His grace in my life

Humility

Abba, Father, Almighty

His strength is made perfect in weakness

His strength is made perfect in weakness

Verse:

Live in His will

Be fulfilled in all things

Have the deepest peace, the highest purpose

Have the greatest joy, be filled with His strength

Travel down the path of righteousness

Life is greater

When you humbly walk with Him

So much greater

When you have a humble heart

Chorus:

Humility

Shows when He has a hold on me

Spirituality

Needs His grace in my life

Humility

Abba, Father, Almighty

His strength is made perfect in weakness

His strength is made perfect in weakness

Don't Turn Away (11/12/2008)

Verse:

There are days

When I don't feel like talking

Talking with you and then

I don't feel like walking

Walking the way, I should

No wonder why I'm inside out

No wonder why There's a drought

And there's no joy where I go

Chorus:

Don't turn away

Don't turn your back on the Lord

Who has given you hope?

Don't turn away

Don't turn away from Him

Who gives life forever more?

Loves you without ending

No matter if you are rich or poor

He has great understanding

Verse:

There are days

When I don't feel like praying

Asking for help and then

I don't feel like serving

Going to your house each day

I don't like the music they play

I'm going to worship you anyway

Sing your praises and bless your name

Chorus:

Don't turn away

Don't turn your back on the Lord

Who has given you hope?

Don't turn away

Don't turn away from Him

Who gives life forever more?

Loves you without ending

No matter if you are rich or poor

He has great understanding

Leave It at The Cross (2/20/2009)

Verse:

Close your eyes pray in His name

Bow your head find peace in your heart

Wait and be still on your knees

In the fragrance of worship

Deep inside cry out to Him

Give your life to His will

Chorus:

Lay it at the foot of the cross

Where our Savior gave for our cause

Where He gave it all to you

And we didn't have to do a thing

Leave it at the foot of the cross

Leave a message of faith and love

Let Him know your praise and need

And give it all to him

Leave it at the cross

Leave it at the cross

PRAYER TO MY ABBA FATHER GOD

Verse:

You have been in this place for too long

But with His grace, live in His rest

Walk in peace in your daily life

Eyes wide open to see

His wisdom guides our feet on the path

Rejoice in His goodness for us

Share the bread and wine in communion

Chorus:

Lay it at the foot of the cross

Where our Savior gave for our cause

Where He gave it all to you

And we didn't have to do a thing

Leave it at the foot of the cross

Leave a message of faith and love

Let Him know your praise and need

And give it all to him

Leave it at the cross

Leave it at the cross

I Can Forgive You Now (4/6/2009)

Verse:

Forgave you and released my pride

That's what my Father said to do

Forgive those you hold a grudge against

So your Father in heaven will forgive you

Keep us forgiven and forgiving others

Keep us safe from our selfishness

Chorus:

I can forgive you now

For my Father came and showed me how

Be humble let me change your heart

I forgave you for so much more

I can forgive you now

Because I pray each day on my knees and bow

To my Father who shows me how

To forgive with His kind of love

Verse:

How many times should I forgive

Every time you are asked for forgiveness

Pray for those who hurt you

Do good to those who hate you

Bless those who curse your name

Love you enemies

Chorus:

I can forgive you now

For my Father came and showed me how

Be humble let me change your heart

I forgave you for so much more

I can forgive you now

Because I pray each day on my knees and bow

To my Father who shows me how

To forgive with His kind of love

Summary

Prayer is the medicine we turn to when the wheels are coming off the wagon. When we are in danger, fear kicks in and our spirit turns to our Abba Father God to ease the anxiety. We cry out and ask God to help us in that moment. But as soon as the anxiety and fear subside, we forget about the need for God. No matter if we are in the gratitude, wandering, or be still stage of our experience, †the need for our Abba Father God is essential. I can only speak from experience that life without my Abba Father God is empty and void of purpose. Romans 8:28 And we know that in all things God works for the good for those who love home, who have been called according to his purpose. There is even more goodness that comes from prayer as written in Romans 8:26-27 In the same way the Spirit helps us in our weakness. We do not know what to pray for, but the Spirit himself intercedes in groans for us, with words that we cannot express. And he searches our hearts and knows the mind of the Spirit, because the Spirit intercedes for the Saints according to God's will.

God's grace allows us to live in the mistakes of the wandering spirit, the humility of gratitude, and the quiet when we are still in God's rest. He strengthens us to be humble and trust that our Abba Father God will be more than enough in good and bad times. We connect to God's grace in the midst of difficulties by transforming behaviors to match 1 Thessalonians 5:16-18 Be joyful always, pray continuously; give thanks in all circumstances, for it is God's will for you in Christ Jesus. We have an advocate that will change us to the end of time. Romans 8:31 What, then, shall we say in response to this? If God is for us, who can be against us? I tell you that it is easy to fall from the will of God if you are not asking, expecting, receiving, and responding. Hang in there, pray, and things will be OK.

About The Author

Dr. Dave Cornelius is an aspiring servant leader with gratitude for God's grace and mercy. Dr. Dave is the founder of 5 Saturdays, a program empowering students to become leaders in business and Science, Technology, Engineering, Agile, and Math (STEAM) fields. You can learn more about the 5 Saturdays education outreach program at https://5Saturdays.org. He is a man of faith, husband, and dad, and is active in both his local and global communities. Dr. Dave believes we can make a difference by sharing our cognitive surplus and experiences with our families, people in the community, and colleagues at work.

Prior works include the book *Transforming Your Leadership Character: The Lean Thinking and Agility Way and Elastic Minds: What are you thinking?* found on Amazon.com.

A complimentary tool is his innovative knowledge cards called "AgilityLeaderShift." The Agility Leader Shift knowledge cards are available on www.AgilityLeaderShift.com. Find his blogs on www.KnolShare.org.

$5.99

ISBN 978-0-9963936-2-1

50599

Made in the USA

Tucson, AZ

January 2019

www.ingramcontent.com/pod-product-compliance
Lightning Source LLC
Chambersburg PA
CBHW021129020426
42331CB00005B/685